There Was an Old Man...

A Collection of Limericks

BY EDWARD LEAR
ILLUSTRATED BY MICHÈLE LEMIEUX

Kids Can Press Ltd., Toronto

Watercolours were used for the full-colour art. Limericks are set in 13-point Italian Garamond.

Co-published with Morrow Junior Books, a division of William Morrow and Company, Inc., New York.
First Canadian edition published 1994

Canadian Cataloguing in Publication Data

Lear, Edward, 1812–1888
There was an old man: a collection of limericks

ISBN 1-55074-213-2

1. Limericks, Juvenile. I. Lemieux, Michèle. II. Title.

PR4879.L2A6   1994   j821'.8   C94-930755-6

With kind appreciation to Morrow Junior Books, William Morrow and Company, Inc., New York,
for their help in the production of the Canadian edition.

Kids Can Press Ltd.
29 Birch Avenue
Toronto, Ontario, Canada
M4V 1E2

Printed and bound in Hong Kong

94 0 9 8 7 6 5 4 3 2

To my old friend Miloš

There was an Old Man with a nose,
Who said, "If you choose to suppose
That my nose is too long, you are certainly wrong!"
That remarkable man with a nose.

There was an Old Person of Dutton,
Whose head was as small as a button:
So to make it look big, he purchased a wig,
And rapidly rushed about Dutton.

There was an Old Man with a flute.
A serpent ran into his boot;
But he played day and night, till the serpent took flight,
And avoided that man with a flute.

There was an Old Man who supposed,
That the street door was partially closed;
But some very large rats, ate his coats and his hats,
While that futile old gentleman dozed.

There was a Young Lady of Firle,
Whose hair was addicted to curl;
It curled up a tree, and all over the sea,
That expansive Young Lady of Firle.

There was an Old Man of Nepaul,
From his horse had a terrible fall;
But, though split quite in two, by some very strong glue,
They mended that man of Nepaul.

There was an Old Man of Dunluce,
Who went out to sea on a goose.
When he'd gone out a mile, he observ'd with a smile,
"It is time to return to Dunluce."

There was an Old Person of Tring,
Who embellished his nose with a ring;
He gazed at the moon, every evening in June,
That ecstatic Old Person of Tring.

There was a Young Lady of Norway,
Who casually sat in a doorway;
When the door squeezed her flat, she exclaimed, "What of that?"
This courageous Young Lady of Norway.

There was an Old Man of Messina,
Whose daughter was named Opsibeena;
She wore a small wig, and rode out on a pig,
To the perfect delight of Messina.

There was an Old Man of Dumblane,
Who greatly resembled a crane;
But they said, "Is it wrong, since your legs are so long,
To request you won't stay in Dumblane?"

There was an Old Man in a tree,
Who was horribly bored by a Bee;
When they said, "Does it buzz?" he replied, "Yes, it does!
It's a regular brute of a Bee!"

There was an Old Man of Dee-side,
Whose hat was exceedingly wide,
But he said, "Do not fail, if it happens to hail,
To come under my hat at Dee-side!"

There was an Old Man of Thermopylae,
Who never did anything properly;
But they said, "If you choose, to boil eggs in your shoes,
You shall never remain in Thermopylae."

There was an Old Man of Boulak,
Who sat on a Crocodile's back;
But they said, "Tow'rds the night, he may probably bite,
Which might vex you, Old Man of Boulak!"

There was an Old Man of Kamschatka,
Who possessed a remarkably fat cur.
His gait and his waddle were held as a model
To all the fat dogs in Kamschatka.

There was an Old Man of the Hague,
Whose ideas were excessively vague;
He built a balloon, to examine the moon,
That deluded Old Man of the Hague.

There was a Young Lady whose bonnet
Came untied when the birds sat upon it;
But she said, "I don't care! All the birds in the air
Are welcome to sit on my bonnet!"

There was an Old Man of Coblenz,
The length of whose legs was immense;
He went with one prance, from Turkey to France,
That surprising Old Man of Coblenz.

There was an Old Lady of Chertsey,
Who made a remarkable curtsey;
She twirled round and round, till she sunk underground,
Which distressed all the people of Chertsey.

There was an Old Person of Rimini,
Who said, "Gracious! Goodness! O Gimini!"
When they said, "Please be still!" she ran down a hill,
And was never more heard of at Rimini.

There was an Old Person of Bromley,
Whose ways were not cheerful or comely;
He sat in the dust, eating spiders and crust,
That unpleasing Old Person of Bromley.

There was an Old Man with a beard,
Who said, "It is just as I feared!
Two Owls and a Hen, four Larks and a Wren,
Have all built their nests in my beard!"

There was an Old Person of Chili,
Whose conduct was painful and silly;
He sat on the stairs, eating apples and pears,
That imprudent Old Person of Chili.

There was an Old Person of Minety,
Who purchased five hundred and ninety
Large apples and pears, which he threw unawares,
At the heads of the people of Minety.

There was a Young Person of Ayr,
Whose head was remarkably square:
On the top, in fine weather, she wore a gold feather,
Which dazzled the people of Ayr.

There was an Old Man in a boat,
Who said, "I'm afloat! I'm afloat!"
When they said, "No! you ain't!" he was ready to faint,
That unhappy Old Man in a boat.

There was an Old Man of the Isles,
Whose face was pervaded with smiles:
He sung high dum diddle, and played on the fiddle,
That amiable man of the Isles.

There was an Old Man in a marsh,
Whose manners were futile and harsh;
He sat on a log, and sang songs to a frog,
That instructive Old Man in a marsh.

There was a Young Lady of Portugal,
Whose ideas were excessively nautical:
She climbed up a tree, to examine the sea,
But declared she would never leave Portugal.

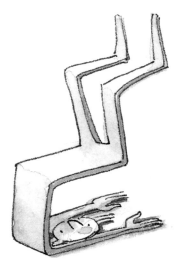

There was an Old Person of Spain,
Who hated all trouble and pain;
So he sat on a chair, with his feet in the air,
That umbrageous Old Person of Spain.

There was an Old Man, who when little
Fell casually into a kettle;
But, growing too stout, he could never get out,
So he passed all his life in that kettle.

There was an Old Man who said, "Hush!
I perceive a young bird in this bush!"
When they said, "Is it small?" he replied, "Not at all!
It is four times as big as the bush!"

There was an Old Man of Thames Ditton,
Who called for something to sit on;
But they brought him a hat, and said, "Sit upon that,
You abruptious Old Man of Thames Ditton!"

There was an Old Person of Bree,
Who frequented the depths of the sea;
She nurs'd the small fishes, and washed all the dishes,
And swam back again into Bree.

There was an Old Person of Cassel,
Whose nose finished off in a tassel;
But they call'd out, "Oh well! Don't it look like a bell!"
Which perplexed that Old Person of Cassel.

There was an Old Man of Madras,
Who rode on a cream-colored ass;
But the length of its ears, so promoted his fears,
That it killed that Old Man of Madras.

There was an Old Man of Quebec,
A beetle ran over his neck;
But he cried, "With a needle, I'll slay you, O beetle!"
That angry Old Man of Quebec.

There was an Old Man of Dumbree,
Who taught little owls to drink tea;
For he said, "To eat mice, is not proper or nice,"
That amiable man of Dumbree.

There was an Old Person of Anerley,
Whose conduct was strange and unmannerly;
She rushed down the Strand, with a pig in each hand,
But returned in the evening to Anerley.

There was a Young Lady of Poole,
Whose soup was excessively cool;
So she put it to boil, by the aid of some oil,
That ingenious Young Lady of Poole.

There was an Old Man on the Border,
Who lived in the utmost disorder;
He danced with the cat, and made tea in his hat,
Which vexed all the folks on the Border.

There was an Old Man of Leghorn,
The smallest as ever was born;
But quickly snapt up he, was once by a puppy,
Who devoured that Old Man of Leghorn.

There was an Old Person of Brigg,
Who purchased no end of a wig;
So that only his nose, and the end of his toes,
Could be seen when he walked about Brigg.

There was an Old Person of Shoreham,
Whose habits were marked by decorum;
He bought an umbrella, and sat in the cellar,
Which pleased all the people of Shoreham.

There was an Old Person of Pinner,
As thin as a lath, if not thinner;
They dressed him in white, and roll'd him up tight,
That elastic Old Person of Pinner.

There is a Young Lady, whose nose,
Continually prospers and grows;
When it grew out of sight, she exclaimed in a fright,
"Oh! Farewell to the end of my nose!"

There was an Old Person of Grange,
Whose manners were scroobious and strange;
He sailed to St. Blubb, in a waterproof tub,
That aquatic Old Person of Grange.

There was an Old Person of Dean
Who dined on one pea, and one bean;
For he said, "More than that, would make me too fat,"
That cautious Old Person of Dean.

There was an Old Person of Wilts,
Who constantly walked upon stilts;
He wreathed them with lilies, and daffy-down-dillies,
That elegant person of Wilts.

There was an Old Man of Berlin,
Whose form was uncommonly thin;
Till he once, by mistake, was mixed up in a cake,
So they baked that Old Man of Berlin.

There was an Old Person of Nice
Whose associates were usually geese.
They walked out together, in all sorts of weather.
That affable person of Nice!

There was an Old Person of Shields,
Who frequented the valley and fields;
All the mice and the cats, and the snakes and the rats,
Followed after that person of Shields.